DOWN BUT NOT OUT
PARENTING
50 Ways to Win With Your Teen

FOREWORD BY TONY CAMPOLO

HOW TO WIN SERIES

DOWN BUT NOT OUT
PARENTING

50 WAYS TO WIN WITH YOUR TEEN

BY DAVID OLSHINE AND RON HABERMAS

Illustrated by Keith Locke

EMPOWERED YOUTH PRODUCTS

Standard Publishing
Cincinnati, Ohio

Dedication

We thank God for the great kids he has brought into our two families: Rachel; Elizabeth, Melissa and Susan—you have helped us become better dads. And to our parents, who helped us make it through the turbulent teen years.

All Scripture quotations, unless otherwise indicated, are taken from the HOLY BIBLE, NEW INTERNATIONAL VERSION®. NIV®. Copyright © 1973, 1978, 1984 by International Bible Society. Used by permission of Zondervan Publishing House. All rights reserved.

Cover Illustration by Keith Locke
Edited by Dale Reeves

Library of Congress Cataloging-In-Publication Data

Olshine, David, 1954—
    Down but not out parenting: 50 ways to win with your teen / by David Olshine and Ron Habermas; illustrated by Keith Locke.
      p. cm.
    ISBN 0-7847-0409-0
    1. Parent and teenager. 2. Parenting. 3. Parenting—Religious aspects—Christianity. I. Habermas, Ronald T. II. Title.
HQ799.15.O57 1995
649'.125—dc20   95-17427
                                                                             CIP

© 1995 by David Olshine and Ron Habermas
All rights reserved
Printed in the United States of America

The Standard Publishing Company, Cincinnati, Ohio
A Division of Standex International Corporation

02 01 00 99 98 97 96 95   5 4 3 2 1

Foreword

I used to have a sermon entitled, "Ten Commandments for Raising Children." Then I got married and had some kids of my own. I changed the title to "Ten **Suggestions** for Raising Children." As my kids hit the teen years, I changed the title again to read, "Ten **Hints** for Raising Children."

The reality is that nobody is quite sure how to do it. The rules and regulations that guided us when we were growing up are often dysfunctional in modern settings. Our affluence requires that we make decisions about the amount of money that we give our children and the use of that money. This problem did not exist in a more frugal era. The impact of television has forced us to deal with a host of powerful influences in the lives of our kids that we neither understand nor know how to counteract. The music that has become a primary value creator in the consciousness of teenagers is beyond our limits of decency. And the changing sexual folkways and mores that govern their behavior leave us with feelings that our sons and daughters are caught up in a culture that will extinguish any sense of right and wrong.

Those of us within the Christian community look to Scripture for guidance. But we tend to be a bit confused. The Bible has to be interpreted and applied to the actual situations that involve our teenage children and we are not sure we know how to do that. But that's what David Olshine and Ron Habermas strive to do. Some of what they say seems like common sense. But much of their content reflects the best insights of modern Christian psychology and sociology. Even more importantly, the authors bring their keen knowledge of Scripture on the subject of raising teens. They try to help us see how God's Word addresses the contemporary concerns about nurturing them.

Historically, America was an agrarian society and traditional familial patterns were commonly known and practiced.

When we moved into the urban-industrial society of the 20th century, those patterns were abruptly disrupted.

First of all, fathers were taken out of the home. Lately, we have talked a great deal about mothers working away from the home. But we do not readily recognize that fathers working outside the home is also a relatively-new phenomenon. A hundred years ago, most American families were into farming —and farmers lived and labored at the same location. Those who were into business also stayed at home when they worked. America had small businesses wherein fathers worked in shops and stores connected to their homes.

All of this changed at the turn of the 20th century. For the first time, factories and offices removed fathers from the home and created a situation in which dads were absent from the household from seven in the morning until six in the evening. The preacher can pound on the pulpit on Father's Day and declare that the man should be head of the house. But if the father is absent for most of the day, he cannot be head of anything. He is just not available for the decision making that the old patriarchal system requires.

In the absence of dad, it is logical to assume that the mother would become the decision maker and leader of the children. Perhaps this would have happened if we had not victimized her with "the cult of motherhood." America has defined her role as being a "love machine." Her ultimate responsibility, contend the "pop" psychologists that haunt us from Oprah to Donahue, is to make sure that her kids know that she loves them. The problem is that it is difficult, if not impossible, to be a strong leader and a love object at the same time. Strong leaders must be willing to risk resentment and temporary animosity. But such attitudes threaten the American mother. She feels guilty if she is not always loved.

Faced with the inherent role conflicts that go with wanting to be loved **and** wanting to be obeyed, the typical American mother has made her decision—to be loved. You can see the dilemma that now faces the contemporary nuclear family. If dad cannot lead because he's not there, and mom is afraid to lead and perhaps incur the resentment of her children, who is left to run the American home?

The answer is simple. It's the children! Our kids control our homes and they have taken over the decision-making process. Parents, for the most part, have thrown up their hands in abdication, and teenagers now rule the scene. Psychologist Erik Erikson said that when teens are forced to make decisions which they feel inadequate to make, they experience high levels of frustration and anger. When they are required to control their own destiny at a time when they feel overwhelmed with the complexities of their situations, they often fall into deep depressions. All over America I see just what Erikson predicted happening. Teens are increasingly frustrated, angry and depressed. Suicide is now the second major cause of death among this age group.

The answer to this leadership crisis in the home requires some innovative thinking for Christians. We know that we must move beyond the patriarchy and matriarchy of the past. We also know that we cannot endure the child-centered familial systems that have had such a devastating effect on our kids. We need a new model for raising teenagers and we sense that this new answer lies in trying to figure out how to make Jesus the head of our homes, and how to bring his will to bear in the decision-making processes that involve our teenage children.

Establishing the lordship of Christ in the home is crucial if teens are to escape the conditions of anarchy and anxiety that threaten their well-being. And parents need help in this task. That's why this book is so important. It is not the last word on the subject, but it is a significant word. It is an outstanding contribution in the right direction.

Dr. Tony Campolo
Professor of Sociology
Eastern College, St. Davids, PA

Introduction

Mark Twain said it best: "When a child turns twelve you should put him in a barrel, nail the lid down and feed him through a knothole. When he turns sixteen, plug the hole."

Whether you're at the "in-the-barrel" years of parenting teens or you're about ready to "plug the hole," this book's for you. No, this book won't produce miracles. It won't change your teen into Mr. Perfect or Miss Wonderful. For that matter, it won't radically transform **you** either. But it will do three specific things:

1. It provides some **practical** suggestions for strengthening your relationship with your teen. The ideas are quite specific. Some of them are just common sense; others are pretty creative (even if we do say so ourselves).

2. These pages offer **supportive insights** for parents. They give hope, in an often hopeless world. They say "thanks" for an often thankless task.

3. This book identifies some simple, yet **significant statistics and stories** that affirm the parent and teen. In some ways, you will find that the "average home" is far more stable than you have been led to believe.

You should also know that we, the authors of this book, are parents of teens—three to be exact. (And a fourth child is nine, going on seventeen!) From our personal experiences, we share the realities of all parents: the highs and lows, the question marks and celebrations. We also share from our professional experiences. Combined, we have either served as youth pastors or have taught courses on youth and the family for more than thirty-eight years. But, even more important, we are committed to scriptural guidelines of parenting. No, there won't be a "chapter and verse" from the Bible for every point. But, hopefully, the truth of God's Word will be obvious. "Jesus in the house" is what it's all about. That is, Christ's love, guidance, peace and forgiveness are what make successful parent-teen relationships.

Finally, it might be useful to the reader to realize that this book grew out of another book project. Our companion resource (also published by Standard) is called TAG-TEAM YOUTH MINISTRY. As a complement to this book, TAG-TEAM attempts to bring important people together to help your teen. Specifically, it's how youth pastors, concerned parents and other interested adults can work, in harmony, for the sake of adolescents. Your teen may often feel as though he's in a wrestling match. He needs to know that you're not fighting against him. Rather, you're in **his** corner. There may be times that you are tempted to throw in the towel. In those times, may you be able to say with the apostle Paul, ". . . we may be knocked down but we are never knocked out!" (2 Corinthians 4:9, PHILLIPS)

So, before you attempt to follow Mark Twain's sage advice, skim through the following pages. Don't be overwhelmed by every entry. Just try two or three new ideas. Give them a chance. Give them some time.

If they **don't** work, you can always "plug the hole"!

1 Rub the Genie's Lamp

Have you ever wanted to know what your teen was thinking? What did he really want from you? What would she ask a genie for, if she had the opportunity?

Group Publishing surveyed 360 teenagers and came up with an intriguing collection, including six wishes that were common to at least half of those polled. The most important wish was for parents to trust them more. Sixty-five percent acknowledged this desire. Closely related to trust were two other wishes: "Give me more freedom" (63%) and "Give me more responsibility" (56%).

What are two or three areas you could identify for your teen, right now, that confront these related issues? More trust, freedom and responsibility concerning his personal finances? His time? His schoolwork? His chores at home?

The last three wishes from the survey can be combined as well: 59% of teens wanted their parents to say "I love you" more often. Two particular ways to demonstrate that love were also noted: 54% of youth wished mom and dad were more interested in the things they cared about; and 49% wished parents would spend more time with them.

It all comes down to two primary wishes. Teens are saying, "Affirm me for what **I can do**" and "Support me for **who I am.**"

② Travel Back in Time

When you're tempted to give a word of advice to your teen, **stop!** Wait until you've taken a trip. A trip back in time to your own adolescent years. Remember your own struggles, the emotional highs and lows and the awkward moments. Recall when you tripped over your own two feet and landed—facedown—smack in front of that guy or girl you dreamed about. Remember when acne appeared at the worst time possible. Travel back to those exhilarating roller-coaster rides of heartbreak, then first love, followed by more heartbreak.

Now, realize that present-day teens face many more pressures and uncertainties than you ever did. More temptations. More opportunities. Their world is so much different than ours. We were **never** their age.

When you return from your time travel, don't say—don't **ever** say: "Oh yeah, when **I** was your age, ya know what I used to do?!" Nobody, but nobody, likes to hear those references to yesteryear. It's unproductive. It's irrelevant. It's boring. Rather, be sensitive to the hurts, frustrations, wonders, stress, contradictions, injustices and joys of those fickle adolescent years.

Think of it this way: traveling back in time can be compared with flipping through the family photo album or popping in the family reunion videotape. When you see pictures of earlier times and events, everything's great! Everyone's smiling and having a super time. But it doesn't take a rocket scientist to realize that those flashbacks tell only part of the story, at best. After all, who keeps pictures of birthday parties that flopped? Or videos of a child's winless sports season?

Make it your goal to travel back in time and fill in the realistic gaps of those pictures and videos. Understand what it was **really** like. Take "Time Travel" trips often. Then speak prudently to your teen.

3 Pump Them Up

Tell your teen how much you love her—but refrain from always using the "L" word. Here are three practical suggestions:

1. Find other words to verbally express your affection. These might include, "I'm **proud** of you," "You're **very special** to me" and "I **thank God** for you."

2. Express your affection for who she **is,** not for what she **does.** In other words, show her your love, even when she disappoints you. The payback for your unconditional love is tremendous—your relationship with her will be less stressful, less performance-based and more transparent.

3. Get to know your kid's individual needs for affection. If you have more than one child, this is particularly important. Be assured of one thing: every person's drive and desire for love is different. Consequently, when it comes to showing your affection for one child, don't think, or say, "But that's how we treated your sister (or brother!)."

As one psychologist put it, think of the need for love as a unique "emotional tank" inside each individual. Some tanks are larger than others; some tanks get emptied quicker. Others require additives. Some tanks run on higher octane.

Consider these insightful words from Stephen Covey:

"We want our children to get **more** fun and satisfaction from the family than from the school or from their peers or from any other outside influence. . . . We try to have regular dates, at least once a month, with each child and do something that is special to that child."[1]

Whatever the case, don't let your kids run on empty. Pump them up.

---

[1] From PRINCIPLE-CENTERED LEADERSHIP (New York: Simon & Schuster, 1990/ 1991), p. 146.

4 SPACED OUT

Joshua screamed at his mom, "Give me some space!" Sometimes it's tough to watch your kids, as preteens, move away from their childhood dependency. Puberty kicks in, and wham! They don't even want to be seen with you in public. Ouch!

One of the primary characteristics of adolescence is the search for freedom. It's a process of separation. Physical and emotional separation from those they love. Do they, now, not love or love less? Not at all. They simply must separate in order to discover who they are. They must differentiate themselves from others. It's a teen's weaning phase.

Oftentimes this means that youth just want to be alone. It's their season of self-discovery. It doesn't last forever, but it can be a lengthy six or seven years. They need their space. It's not so much that your kid wants to be a hermit. He just needs some time to think, read and listen to music. By himself. It's normal. It's standard operating procedure.

Your job is to provide your teen with places where he can escape. His room is the natural place to go. But if he does not have the luxury of an entire room to himself, intentionally schedule times during the week when a private place can be his—**all alone!** Once he retreats into his "bat cave," let him hang from the walls alone. Don't intrude. Give him some private time.

Having these boundaries doesn't mean you must

stay away completely, but rather respect teenagers for some of their personal needs. Understand their moods and personalities. Some teens have been drained physically and emotionally from their day at school. They might need an hour to recharge their batteries. You probably feel the same way after a long day of work. Give 'em some space. It will do them (and you!) a world of good.

5. Discover Common Ground

Listen to the following comments from teens about their parents:
- "I'm not Daddy's little girl anymore," said 16-year-old Beth.
- Jonathan, a 13-year-old, confessed, "We have nothing to share."
- "I'm not very open with my parents," said Jennifer, a 17-year-old.

How do parents get inside their teenager's world? Like any strong relationship, there must be some similar interests between participants. Even minimal. Here's how some parents are discovering common ground.
- Tom and his teenage boys go fishing as often as possible.
- Debby and her daughter enjoy craft shows and garage sales.
- David and his daughter watch STAR TREK reruns together.
- Wayne and his son head to McDonald's every Tuesday morning before school starts.
- Cynthia rides bikes with her two teens, at least once a week.

What are you doing with your kids? What kind of memories are being made? Whether it's hiking, hitting tennis balls or baking a pie together, **do something together.** And do it often. Make it a habit. Make it a routine. And, by the way, have fun!

Realize that your teenager wants, from time to time, to have shared interests. And remember the profound principle: **something is better than nothing.** Ask yourself these questions:
- ♦ "What does my child like to do?"
- ♦ "What does he do well?"
- ♦ "What does she **say** she enjoys?"

Observe. Investigate. Then, slowly and carefully, get involved. Ben likes working on cars, so be prepared for some grease! Jenny loves golf, so get ready to yell "fore." Discover what **your kid** enjoys—not necessarily what **you** like to do. Then do it. As you develop togetherness based on common ground, your relationship will elevate to higher ground.

6. When Life Is Out of Control

"**L**ord, help Rachel this morning. I give you my fears and worries and entrust her to your care." This was my [David's] prayer at 5:15 A.M. My daughter was going under the knife for minor surgery. I had known about this hospital visit for some time, but as the day drew near worries and fears multiplied. What was God trying to teach me?

Bad things do happen. They happen to bad people. And to good people. God sends rain on the just and the unjust. As I pondered my own situation, Psalm 27 came to my mind. What can we do when circumstances are out of our control? First, **we are to trust God with our concerns.** "The Lord is my light and my salvation—whom shall I fear? The Lord is the stronghold of my life—of whom shall I be afraid?" (vs. 1).

Parents have many fears for their kids—fear of drugs, guns, sexual intimacy before marriage, drunk drivers and college, to name a few. Questions like, "Will my child ever get married?" or, "Will my kid know God?" The voices of our culture tell us to live in fear. God tells us to fear **him.** There's a world of difference between those two pieces of advice. As a child I sang a tune—"He's got the whole world in his hands." And he does. The "whole world" includes releasing our fears, surrendering our kids to "his hands."

Second, **we need to ask God to instruct us.** Verse 11 says, "Teach me your way, O Lord." If we think we can pave the way for our kids in **our** strength, in **our** intelligence, in **our** power, we are fooling ourselves. We need a perspective that is wiser than us. His name is Jesus. He can help us through the lowest valley. He can calm our fears and heal our hurts. If you've never accepted him as your Savior, why not now? The name "Jesus" means "God is our salvation." He will save us—from hell, from ourselves, from being destructive parents. Just ask Christ to be the head of your home. Obey his Word.

Jesus does not promise an easy life. He **does** promise his presence every step we make, every breath we take. He wants to direct our lives—and the lives of our kids.

P.S. The surgery went super. Rachel asked for a Big Mac™ in post-op. As I was leaving the hospital, I went into their coffee shop. On a plaque hanging on the wall were the words of Psalm 27. I couldn't believe it. God was definitely trying to get my attention.

7 All Ears

You want a good relationship with your teen, right? What's the key? Giving her what she wants? Why not an all-expense-paid trip to Cancun with her friends? That won't really satisfy either of you. Sure, your kid loves gifts, but that isn't what she **really wants.**

"Okay, so what does my teen really want?" you might ask. Are you sitting down? Here it comes. Ready? She wants . . . **you!** That's right. Your teen wants your **presence,** not just your presents. She wants your soul, not a savings account. She wants all ears, not an all-expense-paid vacation.

To be present means to hear teens out. Preaching doesn't work. Listening does. Rolling your eyeballs doesn't help much. Eye contact will. Talking a mile a minute will frustrate them. Listening to them will say they're important. Not every situation requires "the answer." Not everything your teen says calls for a verbal response. Sometimes active listening is the best strategy.

So listen. Even the Word says, ". . . be quick to listen, slow to speak" (James 1:19). Wise advice. Solid wisdom. Listen more than lecture. "Listen to what?" you ask. Listen to their hopes, joys, visions, goals and problems—with girls, guys, math, science, sports and teachers. Listen to their hurts and wounds. Hear how she lost her notebook and why he's skipping out of a class. Don't lecture much. And stop interrupting.

Help your teen feel so safe around you that he wants to talk openly. How do you know if you're successful? It can be measured by this ultimate compliment: **He will initiate a discussion with you.** So be all ears. If you speak too much and don't listen, your kid will emotionally shut down. So get inside his world. Ask lots of open-ended questions, like "Tell me about your day." Then fully focus your eyes, ears and heart on him. Put the paper down. Turn the tube off. And just listen. It's worth the investment. Have open ears, or your kid might have closed lips.

8. CRYING WOLF

Avoid the temptation to turn every problem into a "life or death" situation. "Crying wolf" too often will make true emergencies more difficult to recognize. Besides, if your kids find out that you fly off the handle easily, they'll just pull your chain more often, to get a charge out of you. And, if you continue your panic-stricken responses, they'll end up selling tickets to their friends—who would love to see a human bottle rocket explode before their very eyes!

Follow the advice of Kenny Rogers, who sang, "You've got to know when to hold 'em, know when to fold 'em, know when to walk away and know when to run." Be sure you know what's **really** worth fighting over and what's not. (Here's a hint: the latter category is far bigger—and comes up more often—than the first category). There are simply too many controversial issues to get worked up over: money; curfew times; dating; total calorie intake; schoolwork; church activities; the number of pierced earrings that any one body should have; and family responsibilities—to name just a few explosive topics.

What's a parent to do? Realize that you have only so much energy, patience and blood pressure to expend. This advice comes from some seasoned parents, who have three teenage boys: "Ask yourself two questions concerning your particular conflict. First, is the issue a moral one? If so, it deserves serious consideration. And, second, what will this issue look like in the light of eternity?" In other words, fight for what really counts; chill on the less important stuff. And try to imagine what a hot topic **now** might look like from Heaven's perspective. That puts it all in proper focus.

9 THE HERO LIES WITHIN YOU

The Orlando Magic have Shaquille O'Neal, the Chicago Bulls have Michael Jordan and the Dallas Cowboys boast Emmitt Smith. We all cheered on Nancy Kerrigan in the '94 Olympics. Heroines and heroes. But our culture also needs some "everyday heroes." The kind of people who don't make a million a year. The individuals who struggle through the day, pay their taxes, live moral lives and try to make a difference in their world.

We've got some people in mind for this position. They've given hundreds—more like thousands—of hours and dollars, and loads of energy to make life a little better for others. They cook, clean and wash. They laugh, cry and hurt. They sacrifice.

We're talking about you. That's right, **you!** You're the heroine or hero we're thinking of. Day after day, month after month, year after year, you get the parenting job done. And done well. It's a thankless job. You've heard that said over and over, and yet you do it faithfully. Sometimes you think, "I'm going to throw in the towel and live in a monastery." Then you push that thought aside. You go back to the routine of serving, helping, teaching, correcting, loving and enriching.

Parenting. The stuff of life. You've had no college classes on it. You work more on natural instinct. You try to follow Truth. It doesn't come easily, but you know that the things in life that are worth the sacrifice have a price to pay. You've invested your life in a child, or maybe two or more. Hats off to you!

You probably won't win an NBA Championship or a Super Bowl. You may never serve in the streets of Calcutta or protect a country from terrorism. But you are doing something that can never be diminished. **You are shaping a human being!** You're making an incredible contribution to the world. And your son or daughter will make a difference too.

So when you look in the mirror and think, "I'm no hero," don't fool yourself. You're enshrined in the "Parents' Hall of Fame."

10 Called to Excellence

General George S. Patton was quoted as saying, "If a man does his best, what else is there?" Excellence is not an act, but a habit. Too often we are guilty of giving our highest level of performance at work and leaving the leftovers for our family. It's easy to see why. We are not paid to be parents. It's a volunteer job! Full-time, but no salary. No supervisors.

In his best-seller, THE SEVEN HABITS OF HIGHLY EFFECTIVE PEOPLE, Steven Covey suggests the principle of beginning with the end in mind. Covey asks the reader to visualize a funeral. The atmosphere is quiet and pensive. Then, one by one, individuals rise to their feet and speak about the deceased person. Each vocalizes an outstanding character trait of their friend. Covey then levels the hammer: **the dead person is you.** What do you want people to say at **your** funeral? In order to achieve a particular aim, Covey says we must set a goal, then work backwards.

A vision never becomes reality without a goal in mind. Begin with a dream. We want our children to say, "Dad (or Mom) was always there for me." Set your aspiration in front of you, and go for it. You'll miss the mark now and then, but you'll miss 100% of the shots you **don't** take. So, set some goals for your family life and start shooting.

11. A Testimony of a 19-Year-Old

Sometimes it's good to hear how parents are doing, "after the fact." One of my [Ron's] college students wrote in her class journal about what her parents now mean to her, looking back on it all. This testimony should be an encouragement to you.

"Going away to college has taught me so many things, not even including what I've learned in classes. I've really learned to appreciate my parents. I guess when you live with anybody they tend to be annoying at times, especially if they're in authority over you. Being away from them has shown me how special they really are to me, and how thankful I am for the way I was raised. I hope that when I have kids I can be as good a mom to them as mine was to me.

"I'm also thankful that both of my parents are Christians, but they never 'shoved it down my throat.' My parents never forced their views on me, and as a result, we don't agree on everything. It makes me sad when I hear of parents neglecting their children, or children hating their parents. I know that in my life, my relationship with my parents is one of the most treasured. I'm so thankful that God blessed me with the best family ever! My parents came up to visit me last weekend, and they've been on my mind all week."

12 Seize the Moments

One of our favorite posters shows a boy sliding safely into a base, just missing the tag of the baseball. The caption says: "Opportunity always involves some risk. You can't steal second base and keep your foot on first."

One night at bedtime, I [David] had the opportunity to practice what I was preaching. My teen, Rachel, was having trouble getting to sleep in a "foreign" place (at the in-laws) and asked me to come be with her for a while. She wanted to have her nightly routine of "daddy-daughter discussion time (DDDT)."

I wanted to go upstairs and watch a TV show, but I didn't. I could have hurried our time, but I resisted. I knew the in-laws were wanting to talk, but I chose the higher priority—I seized the moment.

Rachel and I hugged. We laughed. We had a pillow fight (no wonder she was wound up!). We tickled each other. And talked. Then we both prayed. I told God how much I needed to understand his grace. Rachel thanked him for the good day and the movie we had seen. Those moments were special—much more than watching the "Circus of the Stars" on TV!

Parents battle many things that compete for their time with their kids. Opportunities to be with our children involve a decision. As a friend says, "If something is going to be, it is up to me." Select the important choice over the tyranny of the urgent. Over the easy way out. Seize the moments with your teen.

⑬ Be Yourself, the M.V.P.

Polls show that most teens (74%) like to be with their families and that most (76%) want to spend **even more time** with parents and siblings. We can safely assume, then, that your teens like to be with you and that they like you—even though they might not show it. That's headline news! That should encourage you!

It also means that you **don't** need to be somebody other than who you are. What a relief! You don't need to be "cool." You don't even need to be their pal. Just be you. They'll like it that way.

This doesn't mean you should stop your maturing process. If you have the personality of Homer Simpson, there might be the need for substantial growth. But, it does call you to be human. Honest. Transparent. To be willing to say, "I'm sorry." To be vulnerable. To share your own highs and lows. That's what teens appreciate in all adults, especially parents. The worst thing in the world is to do the opposite: to fake it; to cover up; to be hypocritical.

Be genuinely you. And you'll be given the "Most Valuable Person" award every time.

14 Persistence and Determination

The late President Calvin Coolidge once said: "Nothing in the world can take the place of persistence. Talent will not; nothing is more common than the unsuccessful men with talent. Genius will not; unrewarded genius is almost a proverb. Education will not; the world is full of educated derelicts. Persistence and determination alone are omnipotent."

Derek Redmond was a man of persistence and determination. He came to the 1992 Olympics a man with a mission. There was no doubt in anyone's mind that Derek would win a medal in the 400-meter race. In the semifinals, he was winning big when he pulled a hamstring and fell in agony to the track surface. His hopes for a medal were dashed. He would not even finish the race.

As concerned officials ran to help Derek off the field, he waved them away. The pain was excruciating. It was almost impossible to watch him. In front of millions of people, Derek Redmond did the unthinkable. He slowly pulled himself to his feet and began to hop to the finish line. Suddenly, there was a commotion in the crowd. A man was pushing his way through security. This man was Jim Redmond, Derek's father. He ran onto the track and grabbed his son. Derek couldn't take the pain anymore, stopped and broke down in his dad's arms. "You don't have to do this, Son," Jim

Redmond said. Derek responded, "I have to finish!" The father said, "We started this together and we are going to finish together." And together, Derek and Jim Redmond crossed the finish line . . . to a standing ovation. Following the race, the media asked Derek to explain why he finished. "Dad was the only person who could have helped me, because he understood."

Parenting involves going the distance. It involves persistence and determination. May our sons and daughters say of us: "They were the only ones who could have helped me, because they understood."

15. Love in Different Forms

Listen to the words of a great poet:

> If I give everything I own to the poor and even go to the stake to be burned as a martyr, but don't love, I've gotten nowhere. So, no matter what I say, what I believe, and what I do, I'm bankrupt without love.
>
> Love never gives up. Love cares more for others than for self. Love doesn't want what it doesn't have. Love doesn't strut, doesn't have a swelled head, doesn't force itself on others, isn't always "me first," doesn't fly off the handle, doesn't keep score of the sins of others, doesn't revel when others grovel, takes pleasure in the flowering of truth, puts up with anything, trusts God always, always looks for the best, never looks back, but keeps going to the end.[2]

The writer-poet Paul inscribed these words on love. They're found in the Bible, in 1 Corinthians 13:3-7. Read these words again. Then ask God to help you apply them in your home. It's what matters the most. This four-letter word will change your life—**love.**

Any parent of two or more kids quickly realizes a fact of home life: no two children are exactly the same. No exceptions. Personality, gifts and talents, height, temperament, IQ, opportunities, communication skills, desires, voice, fingerprint, hair and eye color, attitudes. Each teen is unique. Consequently, the way we parents attempt to inform, motivate, encourage and discipline our teens must vary from individual to individual.

Demonstrating love falls into the same category. Some teens value verbal statements of love; others favor nonverbal expressions. Some like to be kissed and hugged; others prefer shoulder punches, a pat on the arm or a back massage.

What complicates our job is that what appeared to be an acceptable form of communicating love with one unique teen **today** might not be acceptable **tomorrow!** So, keep in touch—literally. Be sensitive to what repulses teens and what energizes them. Like a thermostat, keep adjusting your responses to them, as the seasons change.

---

[2]From THE MESSAGE, copyright © 1993. Used by permission of NavPress Publishing Group.

16 Calling Your Kids to Greatness

All of us wanted to be somebody when we were growing up. A doctor. Teacher. Lawyer. Fireman. Professional ball player. Actress. Musician. Preacher. Clown. Artist. As young parents, we started asking our kids the same question: "What do you want to be when you grow up?"

Do you want your teen to live out her dreams? How about God's dream for his life? Do you want your kid to do something great with her life? Make a contribution to society? Make a real difference in the world? If your answer is "yes," provide a place of service **now.** Pretty radical to think about? Jesus says greatness isn't measured by popularity, power, fame or money. **Greatness is defined by servanthood.** According to Jesus, the greatest are those who give themselves to God and to others.

As a parent, you've probably tried every trick in the book to get your kid to "grow up": to make his bed, take out the garbage, clean his bedroom and do the dishes.

Okay, here's a stretching thought: encourage your child to go on a mission trip. (Have you picked your mouth off the floor yet?) A mission trip changes teens. They experience a new culture. They suffer a bit. They evaluate their priorities, greediness and affluence. Three years ago, I [David] led a team of teens and some of their parents on a trip. They served together all week in Belize City, Central America. As they did Vacation Bible School every day in the slums, their hearts were broken. When the youth came back to America, their entire world view was altered.

So try it. Send your kid on a trip to build homes for the poor with Habitat for Humanity. Or check out a local urban outreach. Or go overseas to serve. And—if you want maximum greatness—go along with your child!

17. Connect the Dots

Two of the more familiar criticisms of faith in our society sound something like this: parents often focus on matters of tradition and ritual. They cry out, "Be **reverent!** Show some respect!" Teens, on the other hand, exclaim, "Be **relevant!** What difference does it make here and now?"

In my [Ron's] work with parents, I have found that Deuteronomy 6:20-24 provides an excellent balance of reverence and relevance. A balance of intergenerational conflict and concern. In five short verses, the past, present and future are meaningfully combined. It's like the child's game of connect the dots. The passage begins by posing the challenge: "In the future, when your son

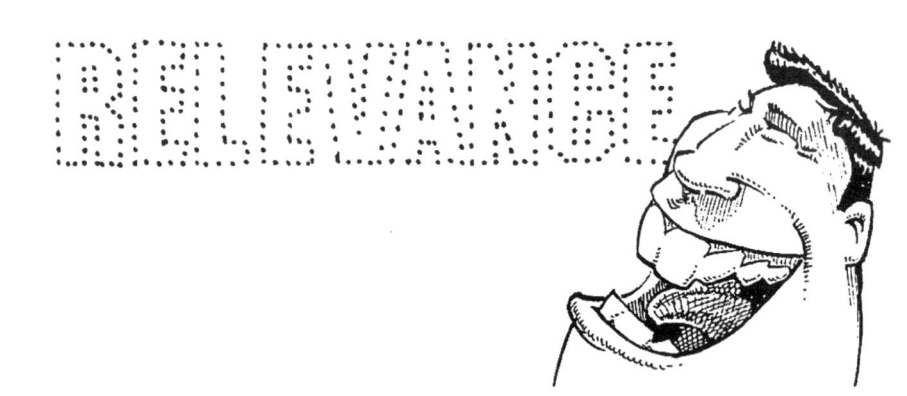

REVERENCE

RELEVANCE

asks you" about the laws "God has commanded you," tell him how the Lord provided for your needs. Tell him how God delivered you from Egypt. In other words, tell him that these **reverent** commands are quite **relevant,** because God still blesses those who obey. In fact, remind your child that the Creator gave you his commands "so that we might always prosper and be kept alive, as is the case today." Notice how the dots are connected (how time is linked).

Using this Scripture as a model for balancing reverence and relevance, ask these practical questions:

1. "What are some ways that my teen and I address the subject of faith?"

2. "How does he (vs. me) raise these issues?"

3. "Does my child feel at ease when raising such issues? If not, what are some of the roadblocks that need to be removed?"

4. "Does my home environment encourage or discourage the discussion of faith and personal convictions? Why or why not?" Explain your answer.

5. "How would I rate my own life witness and testimony, when it comes to helping my teen raise questions of faith?"

6. "What are a couple of ways in which I try to connect the dots? How do I connect between my world and my teen's? How do I connect between human concerns and God's concerns?"

(18) Resolutions or "S.M.A.R.T." Commitments?

It happens once a year. The ritual of making New Year's resolutions. Some call it a wish list. Others see it as a surge of willpower. Most likely, you've tried it once. On New Year's Eve we start contemplating how life can be different on the other side (next year). We think through some of our bad habits. We evaluate the past.

Consider a different twist. Resolutions can be undisciplined or unrealistic. How about getting specific? Use an acrostic, called a S.M.A.R.T. commitment.

S = Specific—Your goal is not vague; it's detailed.
M = Measurable—Your commitment can be assessed.
A = Achievable—It's within the capabilities of your resources.
R = Realistic—It's not a pipe dream. It's something practical.
T = Time Frame—It has a statement about when you plan to make sure it happens.

In order to pull off a S.M.A.R.T. commitment, each of these letters must be worked out. If not, it will merely remain a resolution. We parents are notorious for thinking up rules and resolutions for our kids. But what about some smart goals? Here are some to chew on. Notice how S.M.A.R.T. they are.

♦ I will take my son out for breakfast on Tuesdays before his school begins—for the next four weeks.

- My daughter and I are going to do aerobics together on Mondays and Wednesdays at 3:30 P.M. for the month of January.

Take a few moments to write some S.M.A.R.T. goals in your relationship with your teenager. Go ahead. It will make a new year.

I will _____

_____

_____

_____

_____

_____

_____

Doesn't that feel great?

19. "So, What Do We Talk About?"

You've finally cleared your calendar so that you can spend time with your teens. Great. Now what? What do you talk about when you get together? Start by letting **them** set the agenda. What's going on in their mind? In their world?

Don't be afraid of silent moments during your conversation. Silence can be quite productive in formulating thoughts, reflecting on an idea or providing the opportunity to shift to another topic.

A Gallup poll of over 500 teens revealed the following topics that teens most want to discuss with parents:

- Family finances: 50%
- School: 39%
- Politics: 37%
- Drinking: 37%
- Drugs: 35%
- Sex: 23%
- Religion: 16%

Consider their first choice for a minute: finances. How often do we complain about how our kids spend their money? Yet, when do we actually discuss topics like how to balance a checkbook, our personal convictions about charitable donations or advice about savings accounts and investments? What about long-range financial planning, like college and car loans?

Don't be afraid to talk about money. Some of my [Ron's] best discussions with my oldest daughter, Elizabeth, have been about money. We started talking when she began her baby-sitting jobs.

What priorities should we pass on? How about the challenge for Christians to live humble and simple lives—materialistically speaking? You can't begin too soon. And such a topic leaves the door wide open for related issues of responsibility.

㉠ WAKE-UP CALLS

Neither of us are morning persons, so we each depend on an alarm to get us up and moving. Some clocks are loud and noisy. Others have music to wake you. The digital beeping-kind-of-alarm is reliable and not as annoying as the buzzer type. What are some symbolic wake-up calls that our teenagers are giving us? Are we hearing them? Check out a couple of these wake-up calls:

1. DISTANCING

When teens become distant to the point of emotional withdrawal, they become disengaged. The root source might be one of three possibilities: a lack of interpersonal communication, affection or discipline in the home. God's Word instructs parents, "don't exasperate your children by coming down hard on them" (Ephesians 6:4, THE MESSAGE). Why? The Bible adds, "or you'll crush their spirits."

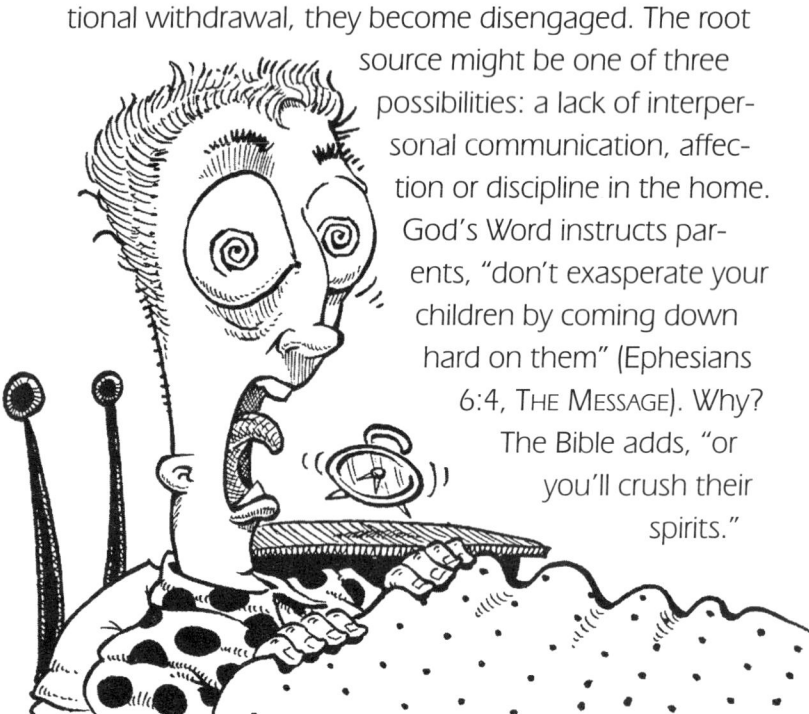

Distancing is not just the temporal, normal need for teens to have their space. It's a continual physical removal. A cutting off of relationships. When your kid hates being in your presence (public or private), his alarm clock is buzzing. He's sending you a serious message.

2. Bitterness

Bitterness is often the result of being embarrassed, ridiculed, corrected or shamed by another person. Hebrews 12:15 tells us to remove any roots of bitterness. As a small root can develop into a huge tree, bitterness can grow in our hearts, ultimately ruining our relationships. Bitterness often occurs when we have some kind of hope dashed. We are let down and disillusioned. This leads to anger, and bitterness follows. Bitterness becomes poison to our soul. Does your teen send off any alarms of being embittered?

Consider four ways in which you can respond to such signals:

- ♦ Recognize that your teen needs consistent affirmation. He probably gets negative reinforcement, on a regular basis, from peers.
- ♦ Realize that forgiveness is absolutely critical. Practice saying "I love you," "I was wrong" and "Please forgive me."
- ♦ Say "no" only when it's necessary. Teens struggle with hearing "NO" all the time. Say it wisely.
- ♦ Get professional help if necessary.

21 "What Does It Mean to You?"

Many of us parents want our children to grow in their own faith. Unfortunately, we forget that one of the best ways to achieve that goal is to be certain that our faith is growing as well. That we publicly talk about our convictions. That we share our own pilgrimage—both the highs and lows; the victories and the doubts.

Two particular elements are very important in this process. First, we must show **ownership faith.** Our teens must observe that we have personally "bought into" the views of faith that we **say** we believe. In other words, our beliefs are not held simply because someone else told us to hold these views—like our parents or pastor.

Discussion is one of the best ways to show ownership. Don't just tell your teen **what** you believe, but also **why.** Let her hear about some ways in which you've wrestled with particular faith-in-life issues—such as business ethics, family responsibilities and civic duties. Be careful you don't always answer more than she is asking. Leave the door open to discuss the issue at another time.

Mature ownership faith—vs. surrogate faith (the faith of another)—tends to yield more ownership faith. As you take seriously the need to claim your own beliefs, you also value the same process for those you love and nurture.

Second, as you desire growing convictions in your teen, show **present faith** in your life, not just past faith. What do your beliefs mean to you now? Today? Avoid references which always bring up history.

Exodus 12:26 captures the essence of **present, ownership faith.** Regarding the annual celebration of the Passover meal, the young child was to "keep their parents honest," so to speak, by raising one reflective question: "What does this ceremony **mean to you?"**

22. GROWING YOUR CHILD SPIRITUALLY

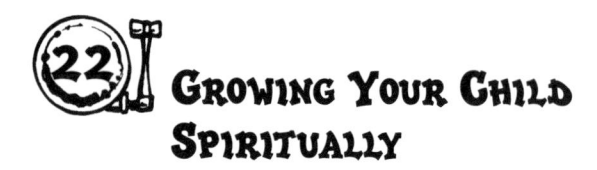

Do you realize that the church **isn't** the primary nurturer of your child's faith? Surprised? The church is there to help, but the main teaching of the Christian faith should come from the home. Listen to these words concerning how parents are to share God's Law:

> Impress them on your children. Talk about them when you sit at home and when you walk along the road, when you lie down and when you get up.
> —Deuteronomy 6:7

The home is where God's truth is taught. It's a natural context. Talk about God when you are eating. Sitting around the house. When you put your kids to bed and when you are getting ready for school, God's Word is to be mentioned, embraced and applied.

Remember that our kids end up looking, thinking and acting like us. They imitate us. Pretty scary, huh? So, before we can help someone else grow spiritually, we must be growing ourselves. Here are a few questions to measure spiritual vitality:

- "Do my kids see me trusting God for needs, guidance and wisdom?"
- "Do they see me pray and read the Bible? Do we do these together?"
- "Do my children see me as a 'giver' or a 'taker'?"
- "Do they hear my godly conversation and encouraging words?"

- "Are there some clear boundaries in the house for the TV and stereo?"
- "Are Christian values emphasized as a family?"
- "Do my kids see me help those who are less fortunate than us?"

Evaluate your growth. Realize that God wants you to be a strong, godly example for your kids. Just live it.

23. You've Come Farther Than You Think

Too often we parents dump on ourselves. We only recall times when we've messed up with our teen.

Don't be so hard on yourself. You also need to see the successes. Think of the relationship with your kid as a **journey.** A trip down a long, almost endless, road. Sure, there have been moments when you've hit potholes. Had breakdowns. Run out of gas. There may have even been disastrous times on this journey when you ignored signs like "bridge out" or "icy corners."

Take a look in the rearview mirror. See how far you've come. Recall the journey accomplishments, too: safely arriving at several destinations together; enjoying rest areas; celebrating exhilarating highway experiences.

Face it—it's been a good trip, overall. Rejoice in that fact. There are many more miles to travel together. So, consider these travel suggestions:

- Proceed with caution, but also enjoy yourself.
- Don't attempt to "do everything" on your trip, just a few meaningful things.
- Look for little signs of progress.
- Put the top down and have a great time together!

24. What Teens Want in Parents

One hundred thousand children between eight- and fourteen-years-old were asked what they wanted most in their parents; these were the top ten suggestions:[3]

10. Parents who are consistent.
9. Parents who concentrate on good points instead of weaknesses.
8. Parents who give punishment when needed but not in front of others—especially their friends.
7. Parents who answer their questions.
6. Parents who build a team spirit with their children.
5. Parents who welcome their friends to the home.
4. Parents who are tolerant of others.
3. Parents who are honest.
2. Parents who treat each family member the same.
1. Parents who don't argue in front of them.

Mom and Dad, you are valuable. Your kids need you. They need visible, intentional parenting. Quality time. They need to know they matter more than TV or a job. Kids need security. Your marriage, when strong, makes them very comfortable. Here are some guidelines:

- Love unconditionally.
- Set fair boundaries.
- Be consistent in discipline.
- Leave a godly legacy.
- Communicate—not just rules, but play with them.

Most kids would die to have parents like this.

---

[3] "Parental Behavior," CORAL RIDGE ENCOUNTER, April 1990, p. 41.

25. Make a Deposit

Every time we encounter our teens, we either build them up or tear them down. There's no neutral ground. Concerning this reality, Steven Covey suggests a helpful analogy. He says we must realize that our kids each have "emotional bank accounts."[4] That is, trust is built much like one builds a bank account. The greater the trust, the richer the deposit. And, richer deposits yield more secure relationships.

How are deposits made? Actually, there are several strategies, and each of these must be modified according to individual personalities and needs. Covey recommends five ways to strengthen trust.

First, we must understand what is considered to be valuable in the sight of our teens. Oftentimes, things that are important to us are not to them.

Second, simply be kind and courteous to your kids. Deposits are made when youth realize you're knocking yourself out for their benefit. Even little things like opening the door for them, or giving them the most comfortable chair in front of the TV.

Third, keep your commitments. Do what you promise. Show up on time. Deliver—what and when you say you will.

Fourth, clarify your expectations. Do your children know precisely what you want from them? Rephrase family rules. Ask for feedback. It's better to be redundant than to presume.

Fifth, show personal integrity. Integrity means "wholeness," no hypocrisy, no exceptions to commendable character. It's more than honesty. It's an honorable life-style.

Finally, Covey cautions against the opposite of deposits—withdrawals. Withdrawals occur with major faux pas. Sincere apologies must immediately follow these failures. All parents make these types of mistakes; only mature ones acknowledge them.

---

[4]Steven Covey, THE SEVEN HABITS OF HIGHLY EFFECTIVE PEOPLE (New York: Simon & Schuster, 1989), pp. 188-199.

26. HE'S ALREADY BEEN THERE

Jesus was perfect. When that fact is taught, sometimes what is conveyed is that all that happened in his life was also perfect. That was not true. He had an imperfect family. He experienced a tough home life.

It's hard to influence your own family. Even Jesus knew this struggle. A prophet has little honor in his hometown. Look at how his extended family reacted to him in Mark 6:1-6. The talk of the hometown was cynical and negative: "He's just a carpenter—Mary's boy. We've known him since he was a kid."[5] Not only did most of his aunts and uncles reject Jesus' messiahship, so did those under his own roof. During Jesus'

ministry, near the time of the Feast of Tabernacles, a number of threats had been made against his life. John 7:5 says that the brothers of Jesus did not believe he was divine. They didn't lend support.

Even worse, Mark 3:20-32 states that Jesus' "family" (including Mary) tried to put Jesus away in an insane asylum. What a family! It's hard to be in a pinch and not receive support from those who are supposed to love you. When Jesus needed his family the most, they weren't around.

How did Jesus respond to such family rejections? He set a great example for us. Your son might not "believe" in you right now. Your daughter might think you're strange at times. Maybe too religious. Do what Jesus did. Don't coerce people to be what **you** want them to be. Let God be the ultimate parent of your kid. Talk to God every day about molding your son or daughter. Don't give up hope.

At the end of Jesus' ministry on earth, we see his mother with him at the crucifixion. Also, Jesus' brothers James and Jude eventually became his followers after the resurrection.

Don't try to change your children. That's God's job. He still changes families today. Maybe even yours.

---

[5]From THE MESSAGE, copyright © 1993. Used by permission of NavPress Publishing Group.

27. All These Changes! ... Is Adolescence a Disease?

From child to teen. Zap! Sometimes the transformation is instantaneous. "Is **that** my kid?!" we might ask ourselves. Often it's very hard to see the resemblance. The "before" and the "after" photos don't quite match up! That's why we all need a crash course on adolescent development. There are a number of changes that happen only in this "season" of life. (It's a six-year season and seems long, but it won't last forever!) What is your teen going through?

Biological Changes
Hormones and new heights! It's a scary time for junior-highers. Some are early bloomers, some late.

Brain Changes
A young person's thought process goes in a new direction. Your child has moved from simple thinking to very complex reasoning. Your kid now is learning to argue and disagree with you. Unbelievable!

Spiritual Changes
Perhaps you raised little Ben in church. He knows his Bible and where to find John 3:16. Now, at thirteen years old, he starts questioning whether the Bible is even true. Is faith really all that important?

What are a mother and father to do?

1. Don't Panic!
All of these alterations are part of the natural process. Your kid isn't mentally deranged (even though

Sigmund Freud said adolescence is a time of temporary mental illness!)

2. COMMUNICATE SENSITIVELY

Tell your teens what they can expect. Explain things to them. Assure them that they're normal. Be sympathetic and compassionate.

3. LISTEN TO THEIR QUESTIONS AND CONCERNS

Junior-highers can be cruel to each other. Let your youth know that you will never embarrass them, laugh at them or preach to them in these years of radical change.

4. APPLAUD YOUR CHILD

Hugs, affection and verbal words of praise will help them on their way toward maturity.

28. Connect With Your Teen's School

If you were given a report card by the school principal for your parental involvement in your teen's life, what grade would you get? How would you rate in these four particular areas:
- asking your child about school?
- asking your child about homework?
- helping with schoolwork?
- attending school meetings or events?

The U.S. Department of Education, through the National Family Involvement Initiative, has recently announced one of its National Education goals: "By the year 2000, all schools will promote partnerships that will increase parental involvement and participation in promoting the social, emotional and academic growth of children."

Even though parental involvement provides a significant component for the student's success in school, trends show a drastic decline of all forms of parental participation between the sixth grade and the twelfth grade. The Search Institute recently surveyed 170,000 public school kids, from 250 school districts, and confirmed this decline. For example, 74% of parents of sixth graders "ask about homework," compared with just 47% of twelfth-grader parents. Also, 52% of parents from the former group "help with schoolwork," whereas only 10% from the latter group get involved.

What are the teen's benefits of parental participation in school? Problem behaviors (like alcohol use, violence and antisocial life-styles) decrease significantly when adult involvement increases. Grades are better. And student participation in extracurricular school activities doubles.

29 DREAM BIG

Do you have a vivid imagination? Do you dream a lot? What kind of dreams do you have for your child? Do you pray for him or her to be a world changer? Dream some of these "possible" dreams:

- Dream of her being courageous like Queen Esther.
- Dream of him being a risk-taker like Abraham.
- Dream of him being meek like Moses.
- Dream of her talking to God like Enoch.
- Dream of him being a nonconformist like Noah.
- Dream of her overcoming tough times like Daniel.
- Dream of him loving Scripture like Martin Luther.
- Dream of her giving the poor a touch of dignity like Mother Teresa.
- Dream of him being a servant like Joshua.
- Dream of him preserving a nation like Josiah.
- Dream of her being a leader like Deborah.

What do you dream for your teen? What do you ask God to do through your child?

Dream big, and let your teenager share your dreams.

30. Q & A Teenage Quiz

How well do you know your son or daughter? Take a few minutes to answer these questions about your teen. If you have two or more teens (God rest your soul), answer these questions separately for each child.

1. What is his biggest complaint about your family?
2. What is your teenager's favorite hobby?
3. Who is your teenager's best friend?
4. What vocation is in your teen's plans?
5. What is your teen's favorite music group?
6. Where does your teen like to "hang out"?
7. What is your teen's greatest joy?
8. What is your teen's greatest fear?
9. What does she say is the best part of your family?
10. What embarrasses your teenager?
11. What sport does your teen like the least?
12. What sport does your teen like the best?
13. What is his favorite subject in school?
14. What is your teen's favorite TV program?
15. Whom does your teenager idolize the most?

After you have finished, interview your teen to see how you did. Then tabulate how many you got right.

- ✓ 10 correct—You should feel good about your relationship!
- ✓ 9 correct—You probably need to work a little harder!
- ✓ 8 or less correct—You definitely need some home improvement!

31. A Teen's "Ten Commandments" to Parents

It's too easy to fall into the trap of always responding to a teen's behavior in knee-jerk fashion. Instead of this popular **reactive** approach, try a **proactive** style. Attempt to build strong parent-teen relationships prior to (or apart from) your youth's life-style.

Teen psychologist Kevin Leman suggests that one of the best ways to promote a proactive plan of parenting is to come at this challenge from your teen's perspective. With this in mind, Leman offers "A Teenager's Ten Commandments to Parents":[6]

1. Please don't give me everything I say I want. Saying "no" shows me you care. I appreciate guidelines.

2. Don't treat me as a little kid. Even though you know what's "right," I need to discover some things for myself.

3. Respect my need for privacy. Often I need to be alone to sort things out and daydream.

4. Never say, "In my day . . ." That's an immediate turnoff. Besides, the pressures and responsibilities of my world are more complicated.

5. I don't pick your friends or clothes; please don't criticize mine. We can disagree and still respect each other's choices.

6. Refrain from always rescuing me; I learn most from my mistakes. Hold me accountable for the decisions I make; it's the only way I'll learn to be responsible.

7. Be brave enough to share your disappointments, thoughts and feelings with me. I'm never too old to be told I'm loved.

8. Don't talk in volumes. I've had years of good instruction—now trust me with the wisdom you have shared.

9. I respect you when you ask me for forgiveness for a thoughtless deed on your part. It proves that neither of us is perfect.

10. Set a good example for me as God intended you to do; I pay more attention to your actions than your words.

Don't worry about trying all ten of these ideas. Start with one or two. Parent from your teen's perspective.

---

[6]Kevin Leman, SMART KIDS, STUPID CHOICES (Ventura, CA: Gospel Light/Regal, 1987), p. 146.

32 "We Were Never Their Age" Inventory

See if you can figure out who said this quote and when it was given:

> Youth today love luxury. They have bad manners, contempt for authority, no respect for older people, and talk nonsense when they should work. Young people do not stand up any longer when adults enter the room. They contradict their parents, talk too much in company, guzzle their food, lay their legs on the table, and tyrannize their elders.

OK, who said this? Someone in our decade? Nope. In our century? Wrong again. These words were spoken approximately 500 B.C. in Athens, Greece. The spokesperson? Socrates, indicting the youth of his day.

Moving from adolescence into adulthood is scary. Insecurity, changes, pressure and fears. Times have changed since we were teenagers. Less contact with grandparents. Upward mobility. More single parents. More divorce. Blended families have increased. Information overload. Technology gone crazy. More choices. More entertainment. More killings. Less family time. Things are **so** different now, as the saying goes: "We were **never** their age."

Take this inventory to strengthen your relationship with your child. Then select two or three questions and really concentrate on your answers.

1. "What positive ways can I contribute to my teen(s) in a negative world?"

2. "How can my teenager and I handle conflict together?"

3. "How can I help my teen make good decisions about drinking and drugs? Sexuality?"

4. "What can I do when my teen refuses to be involved in family events?"

5. "How can I equip my teen to be a responsible person?"

6. "How should I respond to my kid's friends, clothing and music?"

7. "How can I help my teenager improve his self-image?"

8. "How can our family grow spiritually, in practical terms?"

33. "Read" Your Teen

One of the best ways to know teens is to "read" their nonverbal communication. Without saying a single word, they "say" a ton, every minute of the day. It's a language all of its own. Read their facial expressions. What do you see: Sadness? Joy? Disgust? Frustration? Confusion? Reading these expressions allows us to ask pertinent questions, like "How was your day? It looks like you've had a tough one."

Read their voice—not just **what** they say but **how** they say it. Nonverbal communication includes tone of voice, volume and inflection of speech. The phrase "actions speak louder than words" rings true. Watch and listen for signs of sarcasm. Or victory.

Personalities and circumstances change from teen to teen, but here are some general guidelines. What is your child "saying" through these nonverbal signs?

♦ Eye Contact—Does he usually look into others' eyes or avoid them?

♦ Posture—Does he lean toward others, in confidence, or away from them? Is she relaxed or tense?

♦ Touching—When appropriate, does he touch others or not? Does he mind being touched?

♦ Gestures—Does she use her entire body to communicate warmth and openness or is she guarded and closed with her hand motions?

Nonverbal language is a window to the soul. How does your teen's soul look today?

34. Influential People

As a teen, who touched your life? Who influenced you? Who shaped the values you held?

Typically, teens look up to adults for this type of influence—life-sculpting influence. Who are the adults in your teen's life? Whom does he talk about? Whom does she take the time to listen to? Whom does he dress like? Speak like? Whom does she want to be like? Why? Sure, these heroes and heroines change for them—sometimes overnight. But it's important to stay in touch with these models.

Basically there are two kinds of models: those "out there"—on CDs or the big screen, and those "right here"—real, flesh-and-blood people actually in their daily lives. Check out those who fill both categories for your teen. Who are they? Are they the kind of people that are a good influence for your child? If not, help your teen spend time with those who **are** healthy models. For example, invest in the kind of music of the "out there" musicians that would be good for your kid. Pay for the concert tickets, now and then, when good models are in town.

Also, expose your teen to the "right here" people more. Let him see these folks in a variety of settings. Help her get "up front and personal," in order to check out their respected values. In order to emulate them.

35. TEEN MYTHOLOGY AND DRIVING

David Elkind, expert in child and teen psychology, reminds us that teens go through very difficult times of self-esteem and identity. Specifically, young teens begin this struggle because they can now think abstractly. This means, for instance, that they are able to think hypothetically—to picture what an "ideal teen" looks like. And, obviously, **they** don't measure up.

Because of this change in their lives, Elkind says that teens tell themselves two particular myths.[7] The first misbelief could be summarized, "everybody's watching me." Elkind calls it the imaginary audience. Kids believe they're always on center stage. Often, this causes them to focus inwardly, to criticize themselves for not being perfect.

The second myth is represented by the phrase "I'm the only one." Whereas the first myth magnifies self-consciousness, this one overemphasizes isolationism. Each teen thinks he is unique. "Nobody in the entire world has ever experienced the hardships of life like **I** have," he tells himself. Again, he realizes he falls short of the standards of the "ideal youth."

Cliff Schimmels, a seasoned parent of teens and a veteran of youth work, shares the "secret weapon" he used when his own kids were struggling with such identity crises. "I find a vacant parking lot somewhere, and teach them how to drive. You would be amazed how much thirty minutes at the wheel in an isolated parking lot can do for a thirteen-year-old's morale. I haven't resolved the problem. He isn't any more socially accepted, although he may brag about his driving skills all over school. But I have given him a glimpse of what life is going to be like once he gets through this time, and that seems to help."[8]

When my [Ron's] daughter, Elizabeth, learned to drive, it was definitely a big deal. "Bugging" her mom or me was a daily experience: "Can we practice today? When can we go out? How 'bout before supper?" You could always tell a "good driving" day for Elizabeth. Her face would show it. Her tone of voice was up a notch or two! (Learning to drive was one thing. Learning to use a clutch increased the difficulty a hundredfold!)

Don't underestimate the connections between teen accomplishments and self-esteem. They're powerful!

---

[7] David Elkind, ALL GROWN UP AND NO PLACE TO GO (Reading, MA: Addison-Wesley, 1984), p. 33.
[8] Cliff Schimmels, WHEN JUNIOR HIGHS INVADE YOUR HOME (Old Tappan, NJ: Revell, 1984), p. 40.

36 No Contest

The Search Institute conducted an exhaustive study of more than 8,000 young teens and more than 10,000 parents of teens. Teens from fifth to ninth grade were asked, "When trouble comes, whom do you turn to? To whom do you look for advice? Who can get you out of a jam?" **Parents won,** hands down. No contest!

Combining all scores from six categories, parents triumphed over the peers of their kids. Ninth-graders would turn to friends 26% of the time, but would seek help from their parents 40% of the time. In an even more remarkable contrast, fifth-graders would look to their peers just 11% of the time for help, but expect parents to bail them out a whopping 54%!

Teens were given the following options of help: parent; friend; adult friend; relative; clergy; teacher or nobody at all. The categories of "help" included:

- trouble in school—teens would call on their parents (51%) vs. their peers (17%)
- how to handle personal feelings—parents (48%) to peers (24%)
- guilt feelings—38% to 25%, parents over peers.

The final, composite score of all ages and all categories: 48% to 18%, parents whipped peers.

It's not even close. Parents are tops! Pretty reassuring, huh? You're more important than you may realize. When the chips are down, your kids look to you. They know they can count on you. You're #1 in the nation.

37 Rhythm of Family Traditions

Traditions. They are the essence of family life. What traditions are you providing for your family? Here are some ideas to consider:

- Try to eat together, as a family, as much as possible. Take the phone off the hook during meals.
- Plan a once-a-month outing. How about a "date" with each of your kids?
- Play a sport together. Or, go to a concert.
- Determine what you like to do together, find a day and do it often.
- Eat breakfast out at McDonald's or International House of Pancakes, before school.
- Consistently read Scripture together and talk about relevant issues.
- Have reunions with extended family.
- Watch a good video together and talk about its meaning.
- Be sure that your kids understand your beliefs, especially when you celebrate religious traditions.

A teacher we know wears a sweatshirt, with these appropriate words: "A hundred years from now it will not matter what my bank account was, the sort of house I lived in, or the kind of car I drove, but the world may be different because I was important in the life of a child!"

Be **important** in the life of your child. Provide memories for your teen that will leave a lasting impression.

38 Parents' Big Instructions

In the last few years, a number of books have appeared with titles like, LIFE'S LITTLE INSTRUCTION BOOK and GOD'S LITTLE INSTRUCTION BOOK. These marvelous manuscripts list pithy sayings that ring true for the reader. Here's some food for thought for you:

- Let your teen experience the consequences of her decisions.
- Don't be afraid of change; be afraid of ruts.
- Alter your statements from "you" to "I" messages; be personal.
- Realize that lessons in life are more "caught than taught."
- Enable your teen to find solutions to his own problems.
- Your goal is to ultimately let go of your teen, not to control him.
- One day your teenager will be your adult friend.
- Continual criticism cuts your child's self-worth; affirmation builds a strong image.
- Give at least three hugs a day, maybe more.
- Find creative ways of showing your love.
- Buy a SEVENTEEN, YM, SASSY OR THRASHER magazine to stay current with what teens are going through.
- Your kid needs a safe place to regain hope. Make it your home.
- Keep the TV off as much as possible.
- Involve your teen in serving others.

- Ask your teen questions that provoke intelligent answers.
- If you make a promise, keep it.
- Do one activity a week with your child.
- Only fight over nonnegotiable issues. Be cautious of winning the battle but losing the war.
- Make sure your teen has connections with the extended family.
- Seek to understand your child's world, rather than being a know-it-all.
- Help your teen grow in his faith—what **he** believes.
- Have as much fun as possible with your family.

39 SET FAIR LIMITS

Rules and discipline are never easy to discuss, but if you want to show tough love to your kids, these subjects must surface. There are different types of family rules and discipline. Some rules—like laws in society stand for safety: "Buckle your seat belts" is as sensible as telling your kids not to drink and drive—or to ride with those who do.

Other family rules are fuzzier—and, therefore, more controversial. As much as possible, bring young teens into the policymaking process. Get their input on issues like curfew times, places to go and how to spend their money. Involving teens goes a long way in promoting good communication, mutual respect, responsibility, trust, obedience and ownership of family rules. Sometimes this process of youth participation breaks down, however, because too much is expected of the teen's role. They may need firmer, loving reinforcement of a family rule from someone more objective than themselves. An external, accountability partner.

I [Ron] knew of parents who realized their teen had unwittingly taken advantage of certain privileges. As a result, school grades had plummeted. Upon loving confrontation and additional family directives to bring grades back up, the parents were shocked to hear their sixteen-year-old respond, "I was hoping you'd do that. I was hoping you would make some helpful rules like these to get me back on track."

40 Did You Know?

How well do you know your teen? What about your knowledge of the youth culture? Here are some timeless truths for your consideration:

- Teenagers are neither children nor adults; they exist in a time of uncertainty and confusion.
- Parents, along with teens, are also going through some type of crisis, with their own "midlife" issues.
- Children are a gift from God (Psalm 127:3-5).
- Parents are the primary nurturers of kids (Deuteronomy 6:6, 7)
- The culture opposes your values (Romans 12:1, 2).
- Your teen wants autonomy and responsibility, but also needs guidelines.
- Your teen is seeking answers to life's toughest questions.
- Teens face more pressures today than ever before.
- If you feel over your head, get some help from a friend, your church or some other professional.
- The views of the media have a profound influence on your kids.
- Television, MTV, radio and videos are changing the lives of teenagers—usually for the worse.
- Having sexual intercourse is the norm in most of today's music, movies and television sitcoms.
- God is usually mocked through media; Christians are portrayed as idiots and losers.
- Our teens are watching how we live out our faith.

41 Making an Impact

Whatever else may be said about home, it is the bottom line of life, the anvil upon which attitudes and convictions are hammered out. It is the place where life's bills come due, the single most influential force in our earthly existence. No price tag can adequately reflect its value. No gauge can measure its ultimate influence . . . for good or ill. It is at home, among family members, that we come to terms with circumstances. It is here life makes up its mind.[9]

Home is where the heart is, at least some of the time. God created the family. It was the first institution, and it was **his** idea. Since the family is the "bottom line" of life, how can we impact our teens over the long haul? Consider these four principles:

1. Don't underestimate your ability to influence your teen. Many parents have given up on their child; they say that it's too late to mold him. Don't give up. Never, never give up!

2. See parenting as your highest calling in life. Our culture has convinced most people that their job is number one. It isn't. Parenting is tough. But the sacrifice brings incredible joy.

3. Teens look to parents more than to anyone else. Even though your child is peer conscious, she spends more waking hours with you than with anyone else. Your faithful modeling **does** make an impact.

4. Love means spending time with kids. Your teen wants your ears, your heart and your mind. He wants to be with you. So, if you really love your kid, spend time with him. It will have everlasting benefits.

---

[9] Charles R. Swindoll, HOME: WHERE LIFE MAKES UP ITS MIND (Portland, OR: Multnomah Press, 1979), p. 5.

42 You're Not Alone

"**I**t's tough being a parent!" "I wasn't prepared for this!" "I worry too much about them!" Do you ever catch yourself confessing these things? Well, you're not alone.

BETTER HOMES AND GARDENS surveyed 30,000 parents. Asked whether child-rearing is like they expected it to be, 48% of parents said "yes," 47% claimed it was more difficult and only 4% stated that it was easier (the 4% were probably parents whose kids had not yet become teens). Three-fourths of those surveyed admitted that it's more difficult to parent today than ever before.

In another poll of more than 10,000 parents of teens, 86% of moms and 76% of dads testified that being a good caregiver is "one of the hardest things they do." Furthermore, 66% of mothers and 60% of fathers worry about how they're doing as parents. So, join the crowd! You're in good company if you've shared similar concerns.

Oh, by the way, you probably share one more statistic with fellow parents. Twenty-seven thousand of the 30,000 parents (90%) polled by BETTER HOMES AND GARDENS fully agree with the phrase that, even after all its difficulties and worries, **"parenting is worth it."** That's comparable to a decent-sized crowd watching the Red Sox play baseball in Fenway Park. Now, that's a lot of positive parents!

43. You're More Successful Than You Know

In a survey of more than 2,000 youths (14-21 years of age) by Seventeen magazine, several positive views of the family were cited:
- 82% agreed with the phrase, "I owe my parent(s) a lot, since they have done so much for me."
- 75% said, "All in all, I'm pretty close with my sibling(s)."
- 74% agreed that "My parents get along well with each other."

Read those statistics again and listen to their compliments. The vast majority of adolescents are grateful, appreciative, cooperative and thankful for parental harmony. They also enjoy being with their families!

Wow! We don't hear positive news like this enough. But it's true. Want more? This same survey showed:
- only 5% of over 2,000 teens thought that "my parent(s) put too much pressure on me to be popular."
- only 6% claimed, "My parent(s) don't care what I do."
- only 10% believed that "my parents give me money or things, sometimes in place of love."

Again, turn those responses into compliments; at least every nine out of ten kids would affirm: no pressure from folks; my parents **do** care about things I do; and they show their love, not just their money.

Good show. Stand up and take a bow!

44 LET THE LAUGHTER BEGIN

A neat little verse in the book of Proverbs says, "Laughter cannot mask a heavy heart. When the laughter ends, the grief remains" (14:13, THE LIVING BIBLE). It's too easy, in our culture, to get cynical. We become grumpy parents. We demand a lot. We push our kids hard—to be respectful, intelligent and obedient. So we set the rules. And when they're broken, we set more demanding ones. Before we know it, we often push our kids away from us.

How does this happen? We may have lost our sense of humor. We may have become too serious. Perhaps we're trying too hard to be "good parents." We need a new paradigm for life. It's called joy. We need a huge dose of hilarity. We aren't fun anymore and our kids know it. Sometimes our children want to avoid us, not because they don't love us; it's just because we have become so boring. No fun! We look like we've just swallowed some pickle juice.

I [David] once asked an elderly man in my church why his children and grandkids were so happy and content. He answered me in five words: "Have fun. Have a blast."

Delores Curren, noted authority on the home, has mentioned fifteen qualities that exist within healthy families. Humor was on her list. How can we obtain this quality that seems so elusive, usually temporary? Here are some guidelines:

- Be authentic.
- Be creative.
- Set aside one night each week as a time of silliness (planned with your kids).
- Don't take yourself so seriously.
- Laugh about the funny things that God has put into your lives.
- Laugh at least five times a day.
- Keep television to a minimum.
- Develop close relationships with one another.

Just like the old man said, "Have fun. Have a blast!"

45 Faith Makes a Difference

Government is slowly realizing it. Community leaders are taking notice. Law enforcement agencies see it every day.

A couple of years ago, 47,000 sixth through twelfth grade public school students were surveyed. Youth who attended religious services at least once or twice a month (defined as "active youth") were compared with adolescents who rarely or never attended religious services (referred to as "inactive youth"). The conclusion? Active youth were nearly half as likely to participate in at-risk behavior as inactive youth.

Specifically, active youth showed more restraint than inactive teens in a dozen at-risk behaviors:

- frequent alcohol use (7%, active vs. 15%, inactive)
- binge drinking (18%, active vs. 32%, inactive)
- daily cigarette use (7%, active vs. 19%, inactive)
- problem drug use (5%, active vs. 14%, inactive)
- sexually active (22%, active vs. 42%, inactive)
- attempted suicide (10%, active vs. 17%, inactive)
- vandalism (7%, active vs. 13%, inactive)
- police trouble (5%, active vs. 11%, inactive)
- theft (8%, active vs. 14%, inactive)
- skipping school (6%, active vs. 14%, inactive)
- driving and drinking (9%, active vs. 16%, inactive)
- riding with a drunk driver (28%, active vs. 40%, inactive)

What can parents do? Besides getting their teens to just "attend" church, they can encourage youth to interact with caring and supportive people in the congregation. Have high expectations of the church's youth group. Promote opportunities for teenagers to get involved with many different aspects of the church's ministries. Connect teens with the larger community network of responsible citizens.

(46) BE A RISK-TAKER

Helen Keller's words rang true to me [David] one day: "Life is either a daring adventure or nothing at all." Here's a page from my diary:

"I wanted to make a difference for God. The Lord allowed me a chance. I attended a conference in Dallas for five days without my family. On the day I returned to Ohio, my plane was rerouted to Charlotte, North Carolina. Plane troubles forced us to spend four hours in the Charlotte airport.

"I was getting angry and grumpy. It felt like an eternity. Finally, it was time to board the plane. As I stood in line, a loudmouthed marine was cussing, smoking and acting like an idiot. He was also boarding the plane. As I heard him use every bad word in the book, I prayed a simple prayer, 'Lord, please don't let this guy sit next to me on the airplane!'

"I sat down in 13C. He sat down in 13B. Oh great! John began telling every detail of his life, like all the drugs he had done. He yapped for twenty minutes without blinking an eye. All of a sudden, he asked, 'What do you do?' I was stunned. I thought to myself, 'If I tell him I'm a Christian, he'll get defensive or turn religious.' I prayed speedily for some creative answer. I blurted out, 'I work for my Father.' Then John asked, 'What does **he** do?'

"'He owns more real estate than anyone else. He has healed more people than any known physicians,'

I said. 'He loves fishing, boating, sheep and doves, but he doesn't like goats,' I responded. John asked, 'Wow, what's his name?' 'My Father's name . . . is God!' John thought he had one 'looney tune' sitting next to him.

"I began to share how God my Father loved me enough to send his Son to earth to die for me. As I shared my story, I noticed out of the corner of my eye that John (the tough, cool, cocky marine) was crying. 'I want what you have,' John barely muttered. And on that plane, 35,000 feet up, I had the privilege of leading John to Christ."

That day I realized a significant lesson: **Being a risk-taker involves a decision.** I almost chose to be silent. I almost chose to be selfish, mediocre and bland.

Choose to live on the edge of adventure. And when you develop this passion, every day, it will rub off onto every area of your life—especially in your home. With your kids. I dare you. Take a risk. There's nothing like it.

47. THE PROBLEM OF PAIN

Aleksandr Solzhenitsyn was tortured and imprisoned. He reflects in a refreshingly honest and transparent manner:

> It was only when I lay there on rotting prison straw that I sensed within myself the first stirring of good. Gradually, it was disclosed to me that the line separating good and evil passes, not through states, nor between classes, nor between political parties either, but right through every human heart, and through all human hearts. So, bless you, prison, for having been in my life.[10]

Does God have anything to say to us about facing pain and trouble in our homes? He certainly does! In James 1:2, 3, we read, "Consider it a sheer gift, friends, when tests and challenges come at you from all sides. You know that under pressure, your faith-life is forced into the open and shows its true colors (THE MESSAGE).

God says that problems **will** come to us. How are we to interpret these tests? First, we are to welcome hard times. That sounds pretty radical, even strange. Welcome difficulty? God wants us to see trials not as destructive, but constructive. Second, recognize that there is a reason for the pain. God has a purpose for allowing tough times to enter our lives. It is not to make us miserable. Rather, it is designed to mature us. God's goal for these problems which hit our homes is to grow us up.

The kind of maturity God is trying to draw out of dads, moms, daughters and sons is called spiritual maturity. It means to not give up when the going gets tough. It takes the wisdom of God to keep going no matter what. This maturity is like a muscle. The more we use it, the more we will stay in shape. Without exercise, we become unfit and flabby.

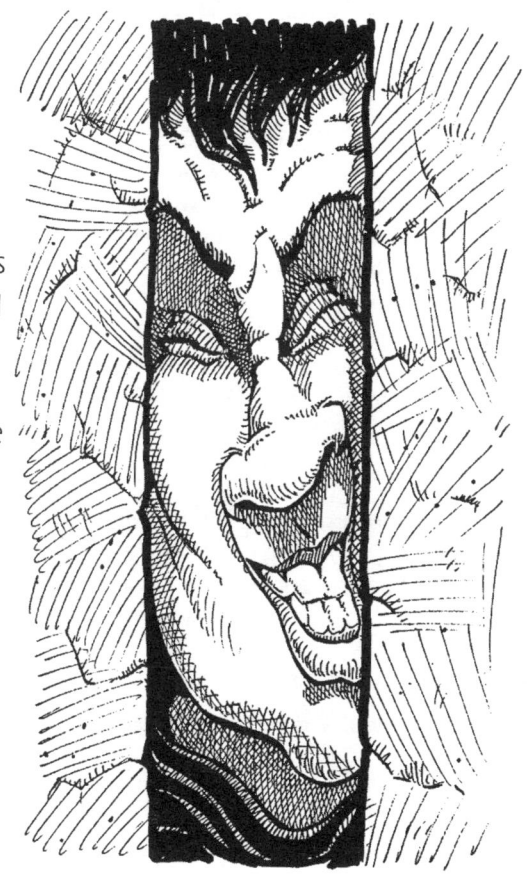

Take a message from God's Book. Pain is meant to mature us. It can bring out the best or the worst in us. The bottom line: When a problem hits our homes, we can either blame God or trust him.

---

[10]Philip Yancey, WHERE IS GOD WHEN IT HURTS? (Grand Rapids, MI: Zondervan, 1977), p. 51.

48. Check Out Your Values

Tony Campolo tells about a time he and his buddy planned to go into a store and change the price tags:

> We imagined what it would be like the next morning when people discovered that radios were selling for a quarter and bobby pins were five dollars each. With diabolical glee, we wondered what it would be like in that store when nobody could figure out what the prices of things really should be.
>
> Sometimes I think that Satan has played the same kind of trick on all of us . . . he has broken into our lives and changed the price tags on things. Too often, under the influences of his malicious ploy, we treat what deserves to be treated with loving care as though it were of little worth. On the other hand, we find ourselves tempted to make great sacrifices for that which, in the long run of life has no lasting value. . . . One of the worst consequences of being fallen creatures is our failure to understand what really is important in life.[11]

We must develop a value system that we carry into our homes. We determine what's really important, what relationships we set as highest priorities. Is it possible that **you** have switched the price tags? Take an inventory of the things you hold dear. Who or what placed the tags on each item? Talk with your teens about price tags. Did your hardworking plans to buy something for the home (a TV sofa) go "up" or "down" in value this week? How about others in your home? How was their "stock" this week, according to you and your kids? Give specific examples to support your ideas.

---

[11] Tony Campolo, Who Switched the Price Tags? (Waco, TX: Word Books, 1986), pp. 13, 14.

49. Get Out of Your Comfort Zone

Peter did what no one else wanted to do. Yet, he did what everyone **wished** they would've done. He got out of the boat. The story is found in Matthew 14:22ff. Jesus had a rough day. His cousin John had died. After completing a miracle, he sent his disciples out to sea as he went up the mountain to pray. Early in the morning, Jesus started walking on the water. The wind blew and the disciples woke up—afraid! Someone (possibly Peter) saw a figure on the water. He thought it was a ghost.

"If that is you, Jesus, tell me to come." "Come," the voice replied. It **was** him! Peter started to get out of the boat. Guess who stayed in the boat? At least Peter had guts. The eleven stayed comfortable. Stuck in a rut. Tied to the familiar. Sure, Peter fell in, once he started walking. (He always gets bad press.) **But at least he tried,** while the others didn't.

Many families today have become too boring, too comfortable with the routine. Stuck in a rut. The day Peter got out of the boat would change his life forever. He found new faith in Jesus. Hey Mom, hey Dad, is your family life stuck? Thriving or just surviving? What do you need to do to get out of your "family boat"? Out of your comfort zone? Start small. Take a baby step. If you fall, get back up. Ask Jesus for help. Keep going. Find creative ways to get out of your boat. And, when you hear Jesus say "Come," get a move on!

50. You've Got What It Takes

Reflect upon the wide range of suggestions in this book. Strong parent-youth relationships come through:
- being sensitive to your teen's needs
- building his trust and self-esteem
- trying to understand her world
- showing you care, through tough love
- effectively communicating, even without words
- expressing your love, with words
- simply listening
- encouraging maturity of any kind
- just being there

When you think about it, parenting is pretty basic. Though it's often complex and difficult, being a parent is also sort of simple. It comes down to common sense. Being kind, being fair, being empathetic. Doing things to and for our kids that we would want done for us.

This is **not** to say that parenting is easy. It's not. Just common sense. So don't kick yourself for being a less-than-perfect parent. Relax. You've got common sense. You've often used it to raise your teen. Congratulations! You've got what it takes. Keep up the good work!

Epilogue:

A Tale of Two Teens, and a Single Dad

You might know this family pretty well. At least three persons appear in this story, found in Luke 15. We don't know where Mom is. We don't know if she is an absentee mother, deceased or what. We **do** know that there is a dad and two sons. There is, at least, a single parent. We know that, today, there are more and more single parents than ever before. It is refreshing to see that this story, told by Jesus himself, is relevant for parents (single and otherwise) of today.

What does a single dad (or maybe in your case, a single mom) do? How can a solo parent run a home when there might be feelings of rejection or neglect? In Luke 15, Dad does something worth noticing for all single parents: **He treats each child with respect, dignity and love. He treats them individually, acknowledging their respective temperaments and needs.** One child might need to cry and the other might need to see a counselor. Be sensitive to the fact that siblings are naturally different. They shouldn't be compared with each other. Let each express his feelings in his own way. Love both in different, but affirming, ways.

Consider how different the two sons in Luke 15 are. First, let's look at Big Brother, the firstborn—the one who stays out of trouble. He's the kind who does his homework and stays off drugs. He makes his bed daily and does the supper dishes. He's already preparing for his future vocation. He looks like the son every parent hopes for. But he has one big problem—he is bitter. Later in the story we find him dying a slow death, due to the poison called resentment.

The younger sibling is also male. Being the typical second-born, he does everything opposite of his older brother. He's lazy, never cleans his room and wants to "discover" himself. He wants to leave home and really live. "Ah, freedom," he thinks, as he plans his escape. According to Jewish law, he was entitled to one-third of the family's inheritance. But, to make this request for the money was completely out of the ordinary. In essence he says, "Drop dead. I want my money and I want it now." By this he shows his self-centeredness.

Here we get to know something about the heart of the father. He doesn't disagree. He doesn't fight. No lecturing or emotional abuse. He lets his son go. The son takes off. We don't know if Dad cried or not, but he was probably dying inside. Did Dad chase him? Probably not. As parents, sometimes we must let our kids experience the consequences of life. It's tough on everyone. But if we rescue our kids from every problem, they'll never grow up . . . nor will we.

The second-born son heads to a "distant country," Luke says. He tells himself, "I'm going to party. It will be fabulous. All the wine and women possible. Let the festivities begin!"

It's hard to have a good time when the money disappears. And that's exactly what happens. The young man starts to wonder why he left home after all. But then again, he made the rules. Now he has to play by them, like it or not. This "prodigal" would have to live with one of the most important decisions of his life. When offered the first chance to make minimum wage, he accepts a job working among pigs. Not a very kosher move for a Jewish boy!

Isn't it amazing how we reevaluate our priorities when we hit rock bottom? This kid is hungry—so hungry that he wants to eat the pods that were being fed to the pigs! **That** is low life! Scripture says he "came to his senses." He contemplates going home, where his needs would be satisfied. So he grabs his duffel bag and heads home. (Most kids that elope, head for the army or university end up appreciating their parents in the long run.) It's hard to totally block out our roots, even if they're not always positive.

God wants our homes to have harmony. The rebellious son in Luke 15 was stuck in a foreign land all alone. He knew he had made a poor decision, so he said to himself, "I . . . will say to him, 'Father, I have sinned against heaven, and in your sight; I am no longer worthy to be called your son: make me as one of your hired men'" (vs. 18, 19, NASB). This was a pivotal day. He knew he had to confess his wrongdoing.

What are the hardest words to say to our kids? How about the most difficult words for our teens to say to us? "I'm sorry." "I was wrong." "I blew it." "I sinned." "Will you forgive me?"

The prodigal has to swallow his pride and change his attitude. Reroute the direction of his life. But how would Dad respond? It's better than a storybook ending. When the father sees his son coming from a distance, he "felt compassion for him." What a scene! Hollywood could not have crafted a more emotional moment. With their hearts pounding, and arms outstretched, father and son run and grab each other, hugging, kissing and crying. What a fantastic reunion!

Among other applications of this story, this earthly father portrays our heavenly Father. Unfortunately, because of this connection, many or us have a distorted view of God. We might think that he deals with us as an unfeeling judge, shaking his fist at us and telling us to go back where we came from. The father in this story gives us a clear picture of the true fatherhood of God. How does God respond to his wayward children? He embraces us. He is not without feeling, but fully compassionate. It's not the kind of picture everyone has of God. In Luke 15, the father immediately calls his servants to get his son some clean clothing, put the family ring on his finger and sandals on his feet. And some good food into his stomach. Dad throws a party!

What an example for us dads and moms! Celebrate with your kids. Rejoice over who they are, **regardless of what they've messed up.** Hug, kiss, show affection. That's the way that God loves.

So, the story closes with a happy ending, right? Not exactly. We are revisited by the first son. He has been in the field—working. This was his faithful, daily routine. No surprises here. He was doing his duty. He hears the music and sees the dancing. He asks one of the servants what's happening and he's told that little brother has sowed some wild oats, but he's returned home. But why the celebration? The elder is ticked off. One version of this story says that "the older brother stalked off in anger and refused to join in." From his perspective, he has been a loyal son all his life. He's caused no grief and heartache for the family. "It's not fair," he shouts, "he splits town, gets drunk, wastes his money and comes home broke. And what's his reward? He gets the best meal in town! **I've** been here for nineteen years, kept the rules and what's **my** reward?! Where's the justice?"

Angry, sulking big brother. He's mad at the world. Mad at Dad. Mad at God. He's been good for no reason at all and now he gets the raw deal. Again, we look to the father for a proper response to the older brother. "Son, you don't understand. You're with me all the time, and everything that is mine is yours—but this is a wonderful time, and we had to celebrate. This brother of yours was dead, and he's alive! He was lost, and he's found!"[12]

Often we forget **who** we are, and most importantly, **what** God has given us. Resentful, bitter people focus **not** on what they **have** but what they **don't have.** The father in the story reminds us of a profound lesson: God is with us all the time. All his blessings are available to us. No one can take that away—that is, until we become mad and bitter.

Whatever is happening in your home, let the truths of Luke 15 shape the way God wants you to treat each other. With respect. Compassion. Embraces. Hugs. Laughter. Tears. Forgiveness. There's always enough love to go around. That's what family life is all about. That's how parent and teen should get along.

---

[12]Luke 15:31, 32, THE MESSAGE, copyright © 1993. Used by permission of NavPress Publishing Group.